THE WACKY FAMILY SURVIVAL GUIDE

by Lisa Eisenberg and Katy Hall

SCHOLASTIC INC.
New York Toronto London Auckland Sydney

To our own wacky family,
without whose constant support and encouragement
we would have written this book
in half the time

ISBN 0-590-44999-0

Copyright © 1991 by Lisa Eisenberg and Katy Hall.
Illustrations copyright © 1991 by Scholastic Inc.
All rights reserved. Published by Scholastic Inc.

12 11 10 9 8 7 6 5 4 3   1 2 3 4 5 6/9

Printed in the U.S.A.   01

First Scholastic printing, September 1991

Does your little brother ever sneak into your room and take your brand-new Madonna T-shirt without asking? Does your mother ever nag you to write that report on the ancient Incas *just* because it's three weeks late? Does your grandfather ever pinch your cheek and say, "Kitchy kitchy koo!" right in front of all your cool friends?

If you answered yes to any of these questions, then you'd better start brushing up on your Wacky Family Survival skills, and *fast*! Just what skills will you need in order to survive life with your totally embarrassing, weird, and Wacky Family? To find out, sharpen your pencil and start in on our Wacky Family Survival IQ Test!

WACKY FAMILY SURVIVAL IQ TEST

Question 1

Your family is off on a long car trip. Naturally, your parents are selfishly hogging the front seat, so you're stuck in the back — wedged in between your brother and your sister, who are squishing you and driving you up the wall with their whining. What do you do?

E. Suggest a family sing-along to keep everyone happy.

F. Invent a rotation system for trading places so everyone has a turn sitting in the worst seat.

G. Unselfishly volunteer to keep the middle seat for the entire trip.

H. Hold your stomach and groan a few times. When your sister asks, "What's wrong?" whisper, "I'm just a little carsick."

The correct answer is **H.** And what's the magic word? Your mom and dad may think it's *please*, but you know it's *carsick*! Once you say it, you'll not only get a window seat, but all the room you want!

Question 2

You've borrowed on your allowance for six months in advance, but you really need some cash. You should:

B. offer to do some extra work around the house to earn some money.

C. try to get some paying jobs in the neighborhood.

D. collect returnable cans and bottles, and take them back to the store for the deposit money.

E. tell your little sister that if she lends you a fiver, you won't tell who put your dad's best tie on the dog.

The correct answer is **E**. If your little sister claims she never touched your father's tie, just insist you saw her do it . . . in her sleep!

Question 3

Your parents have given you the job of cleaning out the refrigerator. You should:

H. throw out all the old leftovers.
I. sort everything and reorganize it by size and shape.
J. wipe down all the sides and shelves with a soapy sponge.
K. All of the above.
L. None of the above.

The correct answer is **L.** When your parents ask you to clean out the refrigerator, just burp and say, "I just did, and everything was delicious!"

Question 4

Your mom has said you can't go out until your room is spotless. When you say your room is clean, she decides to check. Slowly she circles the room, her eyes darting into corners, under your bed. Everything looks neat as a pin. She can't find a single thing out of place! You say:

P. "And I even swept behind the door!"
Q. "See how I reorganized my closet?"
R. "Aw, gee. I was hoping you'd wear white gloves and run your hand along my dust-free windowsill!"
S. "Here, I'll lift up this ruffle so you can see how clean the floor is under my bed."

The correct answer is **P.** You'll only be telling the truth when you . . . sweep *everything* behind the door!

Analyzing Your Answers

If you had the following answers on our quiz:

1: H
2: E
3: L
4: P

. . . well, frankly, we think you're asking for it! And, to make up for getting such a ridiculous score, now you have to *read the rest of this book!*

WACKY MEALTIME
SURVIVAL GUIDE

Basic Rules

1. Always take a big helping of salad, whether you like it or not. That way if you're served something that's just too yucky to eat, you can always hide it under a lettuce leaf.
2. When your parents ask you to help out in the kitchen, offer to make the whole meal. After one taste of *your* cooking, they'll do everything in their power to keep you *out* of the kitchen!
3. When your little brother tattles on you for slipping unwanted pieces of food to your dog, kick him under the table — your *brother*, not the dog!
4. When your parents tell you to get up and help clear the table, say, "But I swallowed my spoon, and I can't stir!" While they are laughing at your little joke, you can slip out of the room.

Ten General Topics Best Not Mentioned at the Table

1. Whether touching your best friend's wart means you'll get one, too.
2. How, when a mosquito bites you, it actually injects a long needlelike straw into your skin and drinks your blood, often gaining four times its body weight from one good slurp.
3. What your mom's gravy reminds you of.
4. How many pieces of rat hair are legally allowed in a bag of chips.
5. How excited you are about the dollar you made today from the kids who dared you to lick the floor of the school bus.
6. Just how large a canker sore can get.
7. What could have happened to the Band-Aid that was around your father's finger when he started making the stew.
8. How the skin on your body flakes off in tiny pieces that fall onto the floor, providing a steady diet for microscopic insects called carpet lice.
9. How many quarts of blood you'll swallow if you lean your head back when you have a nosebleed.
10. Exactly how you discovered the dog was having digestive problems.

How To Get To Eat Out

Let's face it, eating at home every night can be a risky business, especially when your dad just gave your mom a copy of *The Complete Tofu Cookbook* for her birthday. But, if you play your cards right, maybe you can eat out. Here are some Wacky tips on How To Get To Eat Out!

1. Unplug the refrigerator. When the putrid odor wafts out from the kitchen, you'll be on your way!
2. Offer to clean the kitchen. Take out all the family dishes and store them in your dresser drawers. Fill the kitchen drawers and cabinets with your T-shirts and sneakers. If the members of your family are even halfway normal, they'll *hate* trying to drink out of your Reeboks. Helloooo, Burger King!
3. Donate your parents' cookbooks to the Used-Book Fair at your school.
4. Develop a severe allergy to the wood in your dining room table.
5. Go into the kitchen, open wide the refrigerator, stand there looking for a long moment, and then, in a very whiny tone, say . . .

"There's nothing to eat."

17

Best Car-Meal Manners

Even if you do go out to eat, chances are your parents will be too budget-conscious to take you into a restaurant where they might actually have to leave a tip. So that leaves you dining in the luxury of the family car — squished into the backseat again.

For such times, you'll want to pull out your Best Car-Meal Manners:

1. No laughing with more than six French fries in your mouth.
2. No sticking French fries up your nose.
3. No sticking French fries under your upper lip and pretending to be a vampire.
4. No sticking French fries into your father's ears.
5. No putting French fries into the ashtray to be discovered a couple weeks down the road.
6. No putting French fries across your teeth in imitation of your big sister, who just got a full set of railroad track braces.
7. No spelling out !EM PLEH with French fries on the rear window.
8. No more than six packets of catsup for every two French fries.
9. No putting French fries into a paper napkin and squeezing to see how much grease will drip out.
10. No spitting on your brother's French fries.

When a Guest Comes to Dinner

Of course, your parents will want you to be on your extra-special best behavior, particularly when the guest is someone who's just hired your mom for a new job. At a time like this, you must sit up straight at the table and be a charming conversationalist. All you have to do is remember *not* to say:

"How do you get your wig to stay on like that?"

"I'm mad at my brother because he wrecked my science project today, and all the mice got loose in the house."

"My mother's crazy aunt believes there is an alien living in her telephone. After dinner, you want to call her up and pretend to be from outer space?"

"Want to see my wiggly molar?"

"Want to see my head lice?"

Extra Dessert

Occasionally, it happens: Your mom and dad serve something really deliciously scrumptious — like chocolate-chip brownies à la mode, smothered in hot fudge sauce — and one helping just plain isn't enough. You've scarfed yours down in no time; and looking to your left, you notice that your little sister has been busy watching Gramps make his napkin into a bunny puppet and hasn't even touched hers. She's just picking up her spoon.

Now's the time to start a game of Extra Dessert! This is a game for serious players only. There are no rules — only a few suggestions that require extremely skillful technique.

The Appetite Suppressant

Ask your sister if she's noticed that the crack in the ceiling looks exactly like Big Bird's profile. While she's looking up, yank out a hair from your head — better yet, a handful — and lay it across your sister's dessert.

(The only drawback to this suggestion is that while it may discourage your sister from digging into her dessert, it may also dampen your own appetite.)

A Touching Story

(Caution: This will work only with little sisters who are younger than five years old.)

Just as your sister is picking up her spoon, put your pointer finger on top of her dessert. Quickly, remove your finger and place both hands over your ears before the howls of "You Touched My Ice Cream!" cause permanent hearing loss. As your sister runs from the table in tears, say in your most innocent voice, "Who, me?" And when your parents get up to comfort her . . . dig in!

Human Sacrifice

Offer to be your sister's personal food-taster to make sure that no one has poisoned her dessert. Take one bite, grasp your throat, and fall to the floor in agony. When your sister runs to the phone to call an ambulance, finish off her dessert.

WACKY FAMILY
TV (WATCHING) GUIDE

Many of today's families give their kids grief about watching TV. Some parents say their kids watch too much. Some parents don't like the shows their kids watch. And others actually have the nerve to hog the TV for themselves!

Here are a few simple guidelines for making sure *you* get to watch whatever brain-rotting TV show you want!

1. Adjust the HORIZONTAL HOLD knob on your TV so that the picture keeps rolling. The rest of your family will get so sick of seeing Vanna White's face blipping around that they'll quickly stomp off!

2. Put bulky objects, such as books, Slinkies, and toothbrushes, under the cushions of all the seats in front of the TV — except one. Make sure you get the comfortable chair. Then watch as your family members squirm in their seats, finally giving up and leaving the TV to you.

3. Memorize this important fact: The person with the remote-control device has the *power*. Keep the device with you at all times. Sleep with it under your pillow. Wear it to school on a chain around your neck. Never — never — let anyone else touch it!

Wacky Family Programs

Even if you follow our rules for TV survival, your parents may still say you are watching too much. Now is the time to tell them that TV is really all about *families* and *children* and how they get along in their *homes*. To convince them that, in fact, you should be watching even *more* TV, just show them this list of shows:

All in the *Family*
Kids, Inc.
The Hogan *Family*
Full *House*
Married with *Children*
Family Ties
Flintstone *Kids*
Muppet *Babies*
Family Matters
Major *Dad*
Bachelor *Father*
Kids' Court

If they're *still* not convinced, show them this list of Wacky Family favorites:

*Mom*day Night Football
Rose*aunt*
Doogie *House*r
In Living *Room* Color
Twins Peaks
*Pop*eye
America's Most Wan*dad*
Adventures of Super *Mommy*-o *Brothers*
Teenager Mut*aunt* Ninja Turtles
Adventures of *Baby*ar the Elephant
Grown-up Pains

OK, OK, so they're not buying the family approach. And now you're home sick, and the day is dragging. All you've been doing is staring at your fat old math book that your considerate big sister picked up for you so that you wouldn't fall behind. If only you could flick on the tube, you know you'd start to feel better. But nooooooo. Your mom has very definite ideas about the trash that's on afternoon television. Now's the time to trot out the Wacky Guide to Educational Afternoon TV!

Show	*Educational Value*
Santa Barbara	Science: deals with a small town near the San Andreas Fault, a major earthquake area. Related topics: fault lines, earthquake preparedness, developing advanced social skills.
The Young and the Restless	Social science: gives tips for future baby-sitters on how to amuse fidgety preschoolers.

The Days of Our Lives	Social science: compares the human lifespan to those of apes, dogs, and amoebas. Inspiration to make the most of each day.
All My Children	Math: features a large family who work together to make a weekly budget and stick to it. Related topics: multiplication; keeping two sets of books.
As the World Turns	Geography: explores Earth as it spins on its axis. Related topics: eclipses; general dizziness; hair loss.
Another World	Astronomy: explores the possibility of life on other planets. (We said *life*, not *intelligent life*.) Related topics: stars; designer sunglasses.
General Hospital	Science: centers on first-aid techniques for home emergencies, such as washing a cut before applying a Band-Aid. Also, introductory cosmetic surgery.

WACKY FAMILY CAR TRIP

So your family eats and watches TV together without incurring major injuries. But can they endure the *true test* of family togetherness? Fasten your seat belt, because it just might turn out to be a *bumpy ride* when you go on the Wacky Family Car Trip.

The best advice we can offer is, *be prepared*! Here's a list of things you won't want to be without:

1. A small pillow — good for resting your head or starting a pillow fight.
2. A diary or journal — for writing down all the mean things your brothers and sisters say and do so you can tattle later.
3. A pen or pencil — useful for activities involved in No. 2. Also good for writing down new vocabulary words that you might see spray-painted on overpasses.
4. A brown paper bag — cut two holes in it for eyes and put it over your head when your family stops at a "scenic view." This way, no one will know that *you* are hanging out with your family!
5. The family dog — hide Rover in the back and watch for a surprised expression from your mom when, 50 miles out of town, you say, "Surprise!"

Games To Play in the Car

1. "Who Can Burp Loudest?"
2. "Kick the Front Seat"
3. "Four-Letter Word Ghost"
4. "How Long Can You Hold Your Breath Without Passing Out?"
5. "Don't Cross That Line or I'll Rearrange Your Face!"
6. "Guess Who Has Gas!"
7. "Repeat Everything Your Mom Says"
8. "Let's Trade Places!"
9. "Seat Belt Snapping Turtle"
10. "He's Staring at Me, Momma!"

The Ten Most Common Questions
Asked by Children on Long Car Trips

1. What time is it?
2. How come *I* have to sit in the middle?
3. Can't we stop soon?
4. Are we almost there?
5. What smells?
6. Are we there yet?
7. How come *she* always gets to pick the radio station?
8. When are we gonna get there?
9. Didn't *you* pack my stuff?
10. What's that thonking sound?

The Ten Most Common Answers
Given by Parents on Long Car Trips

1. We've been in the car only five minutes!
2. Somebody has to sit there.
3. No.
4. No.
5. (No answer.)
6. No.
7. (A long sigh.)
8. Pretty soon.
9. Oh, no!
10. Think we should pull over, honey?

THE WACKY FAMILY GUIDE TO DISEASE

You wake up in the morning and suddenly it hits you — not the flu, dum-dum, but the fact that you haven't cracked a book for that big geography test today. You *think* Arizona is in the USA, but you're not 100% positive. Hmmmm, sounds like the perfect morning to come down with something. But *what*? Here's the answer in the Wacky Family Guide to Disease *or* How To Get the Most out of Being Sick!

First, you've got to be dead certain of just what disease you're faking, so here's our handy guide:

1. The common cold. No points for creativity; just look pitiful and say "Baba" for "Mama."
2. Mumps. Get the "C" encyclopedia, look up *chipmunk*, then do whatever it takes to resemble that cheeky rodent.
3. Chicken pox. Show a tendency to ruffle feathers and cluck when spoken to; can cause a craving for corn kernels and millet.
4. Measles. With a decent set of Magic Markers, you're in business! Good for long games of connect-the-dots!
5. Scarlet fever. For increased sympathy, leave a copy of *Little Women* lying around, open to the scene where Beth bites the dust!

6. Leprosy. Difficult to fake, since tip of nose, fingers, and toes fall off, but worth a try if you're desperate.
7. Tennis elbow. Will not be taken seriously in some families.
8. Constipation. Where is your self-respect?
9. Bite from a poisonous spider. Just make sure Mom doesn't schedule the exterminator during your favorite TV show.
10. Appendicitis. If you don't mind going in for emergency surgery, give it a try!

Things That THE ILL ONE Deserves from His or Her Family

1. All meals should be served to THE ILL ONE on a bed tray (single red rose in vase, optional).
2. All family members should speak in hushed tones when they are in the same room with THE ILL ONE.
3. Older brothers and sisters must complete THE ILL ONE's homework.
4. Younger brothers and sisters may donate their allowances to THE ILL ONE's recovery fund.
5. Parents should enter THE ILL ONE's presence only to ask how they may be of service.
6. No rectal thermometers.
7. There must be at least one TV on in THE ILL ONE's room at all times.
8. Family pets should be allowed to share THE ILL ONE's bed upon request.
9. Presents for THE ILL ONE will be accepted; ditto for lavish get-well cards, especially those containing cash.
10. A crown or a tiara may be worn by THE ILL ONE, provided it does not cause head pain.

Wacky Family Sympathy

Most vital when you are playing sick is the element of Wacky Family Sympathy. How to get it? Practice saying the lines below until you can do it in a weak and wavery voice:

"I think the TV is tiring me out. Would you mind turning it off?"

"Am I hungry? Maybe I could just nibble on half a cracker."

"Really, I don't mind if you play with my brand-new game."

"Oh, is it my birthday next week? I'd forgotten."

"Oh, no, really. You all go ahead and go to the movie. Don't worry about me. I'll be fine here by myself."

"Chocolate cake? No, I just don't think it would stay down."

WACKY FAMILY-
ADVICE COLUMN

Every day, our mailboxes are bulging with mail from members of Wacky Families asking for advice. We'd like to share some of these letters with you. If you have a problem you'd like to write us about, our advice to you is — *solve it yourself!* We've got families of our own to survive!

Dear Katy & Lisa:
My Little Sister copies everything I do. It's driving me nuts. What should I do?
Signed
Z. Rocks

Dear Z:
Tell your little sister to stop acting like an idiot!
K and L

Dear Katy & Lisa:

My father is always nagging me to do my homework. For my birthday, he gave me a pencil. Can you believe it?

GRRRR,
Ida Rathersleep

Dear Ida:

Sure we can believe it. In fact your father sounds like a pretty sharp guy to us. We think he gave you that pencil to make a point. Now get the lead out and do your homework!

K and L

Dear Katy & Lisa:
My parents don't understand me. My brother and sister don't understand me. In fact, nobody understands me. What should I do?
Sincerely,
Dawn May Kennysense

Dear Dawn:
We can't figure out what you're talking about!
K and L

Dear Katy and Lisa:
My brother's dog
ate my arithmetic
book. What should
I do? Signed,
Al G. Braw

Dear Al:
What are you
worrying about?
Now you don't have
any more problems!

THE WACKY FAMILY GUIDE
TO LEISURE-TIME
ACTIVITIES

Does your idea of a perfect Saturday include:

- sleeping till one P.M.?
- renting five videos?
- inviting four or five friends over to watch?
- snacking on six or seven kinds of chips and sodas?

Do your parents have different ideas? Could some of their activities be described by the word . . . *cultural*? Would they, for example, like to get everyone together and:

- visit an art museum?
- attend a concert?
- see a ballet?

If you see any of these items on one of your parent's calendars, you have our complete sympathy! However, there are certain ways to make sure that cultural activities are something your parents drag you to only *once*!

The Wacky Family Guide to Culture

When you visit an art museum:

- stand near one of the security guards, and call out, "Hey, Mom! What does 'case the joint' mean again?"
- complain of spots before your eyes.
- claim in a loud voice, "I could do that!" every time you view a modern painting.
- complain of dizziness.
- laugh hysterically at the painting of your choice, and when your dad asks you what's so funny, say, "Don't you get it?"
- complain of stomach cramps.
- swing on the velvet ropes.
- complain of nausea.
- yell, "Help! Murder! My feet are killing me!"

When you go to a concert:

- lean forward in your seat and hum your school song.
- pry the wads of gum from under the bottom of your seat and offer them to your brother.
- pull out your harmonica and try to play along.
- clap with your feet.
- fly a paper airplane to the piccolo player.
- jitter in your seat and whisper, "I hope I can hold it!"

When you go to the ballet:

- slump in your seat and moan.
- tap the rhythms of popular songs on the seat in front of you with your right foot, then switch to your left.
- if you find that someone is resting her arm on one of your armrests, put your arm beside hers and slowly, slowly push hers off.
- and the audience calls out, "Bravo!" yell, "Don't fall on your face!"

Wacky Family Cultural Activities
Chosen by Kids

Just because you're not wild to participate in your parents' favorite cultural activities doesn't mean that you want your family to think you're some kind of mindless lowbrow. When your mother and father try to haul you off to a boring museum, symphony, or art gallery, remind them that the dictionary defines *culture* as "the ideas and customs common to a given civilization."

Explain that you'd like to show them some of *your* civilization's common ideas and customs. Then suggest a family outing to one of the following seats of "culture."

1. The Bart Simpson Museum
2. The Museum of Freaks and Oddities, featuring the famous "Longest Toenail Ever Grown" exhibit
3. Justin Fun's Down-Home Video Arcade
4. Yoo-Hoo's Yummy Cakes Factory Tour — Free Samples Included!
5. All-Pro Wrestling Match between Ruby "Rhino" Rhinestone and Tom "Triceratops" Terrifico

WACKY FAMILY GUIDE TO PARENTS AND SIBLINGS

Little Brothers and Sisters

The main thing to remember about little brothers and sisters is that, even though they're smaller than you, they're still trying. *Very* trying! The chart below illustrates "younger brother/sister" problems you'll probably have to deal with soon — if you haven't already!

Sibling Situation	Your Best Response
Your brother constantly whines and begs to play with you and your friends.	Tell him, "Sure, kid. We're playing 'mad scientist' and *you* get to be the experiment!"
Your little sister sneaks into the kitchen and eats your last cream-filled cupcake.	Shout, "What happened to that chemically treated cupcake I left in the kitchen? It was my science-fair entry!"
Your little brother says, "I'll keep my hands off your stuff if you promise me something!"	Say, "Oh, yeah? I'll promise you something if you *don't* keep your hands off my stuff!"
Your little sister begs to go with you.	Offer to take her to the zoo — permanently!

Big Brothers and Sisters

Anyone who's ever had a big brother or sister knows what they're like. They boss you around. They won't let you use their stuff. They make fun of everything you do. And what can you do about it? Not much — because they're *bigger* than you are!

Basically, there are six important things you should do to survive life with a big brother or sister. They are listed below:

1. Tattle
2. Share your things
3. Tattle
4. Tattle
5. Try to cooperate whenever possible
6. Tattle

Brother and Sister Quiz

Just how much more work do you have to do in order to mold them into the perfect siblings you deserve? To find out, ask all your sibs to take our little quiz. *You*, of course, are known as THE SPECIAL SIBLING. If you're lucky enough to be an only child, skip this page!

1. What is the most important room in your family's house?
   a. The kitchen
   b. The living room
   c. Your own room
   d. THE SPECIAL SIBLING's room
2. Which family member is most important?
   a. Your mother
   b. Your father
   c. You
   d. THE SPECIAL SIBLING
3. What is your family's most important possession?
   a. The car
   b. The refrigerator
   c. You
   d. THE SPECIAL SIBLING's mirror
4. When you grow up, would you like to be:
   a. a doctor?
   b. a lawyer?
   c. just plain old you?
   d. THE SPECIAL SIBLING's servant?

How To Score:

Each D answer = 10 points.
Each A or B answer = 5 points.
Each C answer = 0, zero, zip, nada, zilch.

Rating Your Score:

- 40 points — You've got it made! Your brothers and sisters are eating right out of your hand, and you can run this book through any handy paper shredder. (By the way, exactly what form of torture did you use when you brainwashed the little tykes?)
- 20–39 points — Your brothers and sisters are well-balanced and will probably grow up to be productive members of society. Too bad for you! You've got a big job ahead of you. Read on!
- 0–19 points — Your brothers and sisters are selfish, conceited, and interested only in themselves. What'd you do, give them lessons?

Your Parents

Face it. Even if you get your brothers and sisters completely under your control, you'll still have to deal with the two biggest problems of all — your mother and father! On the next few pages, we've listed some methods for dealing with moms and dads.

The Art of Whining

The classic whine is delivered through the nose. Most professional whiners use a lilting form of stretched-out singsong, with many variations in range and pitch. Thus, if the phrase were put to music, it would look like this:

Useful all-purpose whining phrases:

1. "No fair! She gets to do whatever she wants, but I never get to do anything!"
2. "No fair! His piece is bigger than mine!"
3. "No fair! Everyone else has a _____!" (Fill in something you desperately want.)
4. "No fair! I took a bath *last* week!"
5. "No fair! It's *her* turn to clear the table (take out the garbage, change the gerbil cage paper, shovel the walk, sort the laundry, mow the lawn, etc.)!"
6. "No fair! I really did work hard in science (reading, math, social studies, gym, art, playground conduct, etc.)! The teacher gave me a D because he hates me!"
7. "No fair! Tell him to stop pinching (poking, kicking, pulling, teasing, bothering, threatening, copying, spying on, spitting on, sitting on, touching, making faces at, violating the personal space of, offending by merely existing, etc.) me!"

Extra-Credit Whining Homework. Stand in front of a mirror, pout, and practice pronouncing the word *fair* with as many syllables as possible. Don't stop with just two or three. Champion whiners can produce at least five!

The Art of Crying

Even though you whine your brains out, sometimes it just won't do the trick. When that happens, you'll have to resort to the strongest little weapons in your artillery — tears. Crying can be a useful and effective means of getting your own way with your parents. But be careful! Save your tears for real emergencies. Even the most sympathetic parents get sick of a kid who's constantly blubbering about little things, like having to turn off the VCR after only five straight hours of movie-watching!

The best occasions for crying are:

1. When you're really, really hurt . . . or just feeling "sensitive."
2. When you feel really, really sorry for yourself.
3. When you really, really want something.
4. When you're really, really mad at somebody.
5. When you're really, really mad at everybody.
6. When you realize that no one really, really understands you.
7. When you really, really don't want to do something.
8. When you've really, really tried everything else, and it really, really hasn't worked.

The best occasion for turning off your tears like a faucet is when you really, really get your way!

Extra-Credit Crying Homework. Stand in front of a mirror, crumple up your face, and practice crying "at will." You may have to pinch yourself to get started. In fact, if you pinch hard enough, soon you'll feel so sorry for yourself, you'll be crying for real!

Just remember not to stop crying until your parents have *promised* to let you:

- get that really cool drum set.
- put in a swimming pool.
- get a puppy.
- take a trip to Disney World.
- receive a 40-pound box of chocolate candy that you don't have to share.
- have Jell-O for breakfast.
- give your brothers and sisters away.
- hire someone to do all your homework.
- host your own TV talk show.
- quit school.
- get a pony.
- live on sugar-coated cereal.
- keep reading this ridiculous book!

WACKY GUIDE
TO SURVIVING RELATIVES

Aunts, Uncles, and Cousins

One of the wackiest events in Wacky Family Survival history takes place when relatives like Aunt Advica, Uncle Greenback, and Cousin Beperfect come to visit you. "Why . . ." you find yourself asking again and again, ". . . are my aunts and uncles always trying to prove their family is better than my family?"

The answer is as obvious as the wart on Uncle Greenback's nose! When you've finished your whining and complaining, stop sulking and ask yourself this question: Just who exactly *are* my aunts and uncles? When it dawns on you that they're your parents' *brothers and sisters*, you'll immediately understand their petty behavior. They're still treating *their* brothers and sisters in the same childish, obnoxious way you treat *your* brothers and sisters!

So now you understand them a little better. Does that make it any easier to endure their visits? Of course not! In order to help you cope with your aunts, uncles, and cousins the next time they visit, we've provided you with some relatively typical situations in cartoon form on the next few pages. Choose the best response from the list at the bottom and write it in your speech balloon.

A portly, bald uncle is speaking to the Wacky kid, whose response is:

1. I dunno, sir. I've begged and begged my parents to allow me to have one, but they think I look cute this way!
2. Never, sir. My hair is my form of artistic expression!
3. I dunno. But at least *I* have some hair to cut!

A portly aunt is talking to our Wacky girl, whose response is:

1. Grown *what*?
2. You'd groan, too, if you had all these relatives visiting *you*!
3. My, how *you've* grown!

A neat, clean, goody-goody cousin is bragging to our Wacky boy, whose response is:
1. Nyaaaah!
2. I can go to school and get smarter, but *you're* ugly!
3. Nyaaaah!

Grandparents!

In many ways, your grandparents are your best relatives. Why? Because they still think your mother and father are nothing but a pair of overgrown kids who don't know what they're doing! That's why they're usually ready to stick up for you when you're fighting with your parents!

In spite of this, you may still run into some problems surviving your Wacky grandparents. It might help you to learn the good news and bad news about grandparents:

The good news is they'll give you lots of money! But in their day, *ten cents* was a lot of money!

They'll agree to buy whatever junk you have to sell for Scouts! But they'll forget to pay!

They'll always think you're a cute, adorable baby! But they'll show it by trying to burp you in front of your friends!

They're willing to help you with your homework! But they don't know the difference between a computer and a dishwasher!

They'll take you anywhere you want to go! But they'll drive so slowly, you'll go crazy!

They'll give you lots of presents! But they'll all be sweaters to keep you from catching a chill!

They'll give you real candy instead of yogurt-covered raisins! But they won't let you eat it because it might spoil your appetite!

They'll listen to whatever you have to say. But they won't understand a word of it!

You and your grandparents may have some real problems communicating with each other. That's why we're including the handy translation chart below. Whenever you don't have a clue what your grandparents are talking about, whip this out so you'll know whether to laugh or cry.

What Your Grandparents Say	What They Mean
He's just like Cary Grant!	He's just like Michael J. Fox!
A bad apple!	A bogus lame-o!
The cat's meow!	Totally tubular!
Peachy keen!	Dudical!
A real looker!	A primo babe!
Nifty!	Gnarly!
Hep to the jive!	Bodacious!
Don't pop your cork!	Chill!
You're the apple of my eye!	Excellent, dude!
Lose your breakfast!	Barf your brains out!

WACKY FAMILY PET GUIDE

Once you've learned how to manage the human members of your family, it's time to add some animals to the clan!

How To Beg for a Dog*

1. Start out by saying you want something frightening like a pit viper or a tarantula. Your parents will be so horrified, they might even *suggest* a dog as an alternative!

2. Point out the many good things about dog ownership, like companionship, protection from burglars, and exercise on doggy walks. Whatever you do, don't mention anything like puddles on the carpet, chewed-up shoes, bitten mailmen, or whimpering in the night.

3. *Swear* that you'll be responsible for the dog. Promise to housebreak it, walk it, feed it, train it, and clean up after it. (Of course you'll do all these things *for one day only!*)

4. Coyly suggest that if the dog is especially cute, you'd like to name it:
   "_____."

   (insert your father's name here)

If you're lucky, Dad will be flattered enough to buy you a puppy — before he realizes you're saying he looks like a Pekingese!

* With slight variation, this method can also be used to beg for a cat, to promise to empty the litter box, etc.

Training a Puppy

If you've managed to convince your parents that you can't live without a dog, they'll probably have the gall to try to stick you with the job of training your new puppy. Here are some helpful guidelines for dealing with that delicate task:

1. Suggest to your parents that they replace the off-white living room carpet with a pleasant shade of yellow. After your puppy has forty or fifty little "accidents," they'll appreciate the savings in rug cleaner.
2. Help your puppy fit into your Wacky Family by training him to "go" on papers spread out on the kitchen floor. It's a good idea to use old newspapers instead of the important legal briefs you found in Daddy's briefcase. But don't worry! If you make this mistake, you can always explain that your puppy would have chewed those papers up anyway!
3. When your puppy has an "accident," show it the "mess" and say, "No, no! Bad dog!" Try to do this before your sister staggers into the kitchen in the morning with no shoes on.

4. Your puppy has strong canine teeth, and it's only natural for him to want to chew on things. If you can, go to the pet store and buy your puppy some rawhide chew toys to strengthen and cleanse his teeth. If you don't want to spring for the rawhide, you'll find that your brother's guitar strap will make an excellent substitute. Ditto for most of the shoes in your sister's closet.

5. Sooner or later, your puppy will be housebroken and will need to go outside to "do his business." In the wee hours of the morning, when you hear your puppy whining to go out, there are three things you should do:

   a. Pull your blanket up over your head.
   b. Groan.
   c. Shout, "Mo-ommmm! Da-aaad! Puppy needs to go out!" If you're lucky, they'll be too tired after letting the dog out to come into your room and have a serious talk about responsibility!

A "Different" Kind of Pet

If all your efforts fail and your parents still won't let you get a dog, you may have to compromise and settle for another kind of pet. Dollars to donuts, your mom and dad will suggest getting you some kind of boring easy-to-care-for creature. But, because we know you'd rather have something really interesting and unusual, we've given you a list of "alternative" pets to suggest.

Parents' Suggestion	Your Suggestion
A goldfish.	*A South American flesh-eating piranha!* It doesn't take up much more space *and* it disposes of left-over meat!
A canary.	*A turkey buzzard!* Much more interesting to look at! (See above for left-overs!)
An ant farm.	*A black widow spider!* The family gets to watch interesting mating rites, *plus* it eliminates unwanted flies *and* visitors!

A chameleon.	*A Gila monster!* Why settle for an ordinary lizard when you could have the distinction of owning the only known poisonous species?
A hamster.	*An alley rat!* Why, you wouldn't even have to buy it food. Just drop it off occasionally in the garbage dumpster behind your neighborhood restaurant!

WACKY FAMILY GUIDE TO PITCHING IN

If your Wacky family is like most families (don't you wish?!), everyone is encouraged to pitch in and help with the chores that keep the household running.

Ten Most-Hated Household Chores

1. Cleaning the toilet
2. Unloading the dishwasher
3. Cleaning out the garage
4. Vacuuming
5. Doing the laundry
6. Cleaning your room
7. Raking leaves
8. Taking out the garbage
9. Mowing the lawn
10. Shoveling snow

The Ten Best Ways
for Getting Out of Doing
the Ten Most-Hated Household Chores

1. When it's your turn to *clean out the toilet bowl*, just say, "But what if I drown the Tidy Bowl Man?" Your parents will realize that you are far too sensitive for this chore, so they'll rush out and hire a maid.

2. To *unload the dishwasher*, simply place the glasses in the oven, the pots and pans in the refrigerator, and the silverware in the freezer. When your dad complains that he can't ever find anything after you've put the dishes away, accuse him of being sooooo conventional. I mean, where is his sense of fun and creativity, anyway?

3. The easiest way out of *cleaning the garage* is called the garage door. Use it!

4. Maybe you can't get out of *vacuuming*, but at least you can make it pay! Start by sticking the nozzle down among the couch cushions and listen to the *clinks* as you start sucking in all the loose change that Uncle Greenback spilled down there last Thanksgiving. Just make sure to stop before you hear the *clunk* that means *you'll* owe the vacuum repair shop $87.50!

5. In order to get out of *doing the laundry*, never change your clothes. That way you can righteously say, "I haven't contributed to the dirty clothes problem; therefore, I'm not responsible for solving it!"

6. When your family sends you to *clean your room*, sit down amidst the shoes, jeans, tapes, books, toys, candy wrappers, dirty socks, and other accumulated junk you're in the habit of tossing on the floor. When your parents come in to check on you, they won't even be able to find you!

7. To *rake the lawn*, go outside and pick up the rake. Then run back inside screaming, "I've been attacked by a vampire chipmunk!" Your family won't believe you, but at least they'll think you're too nuts to do a good job!

8. When your family tells you to *take out the garbage*, cheerfully agree. Then put the garbage into a "wimpy" bag. On your way out to the garbage cans, make a detour into the dining room. Is it your fault if the bag "accidentally" splits open on top of the new Persian rug?

9. After *mowing the lawn* for exactly 30 seconds, pretend to get a bee stuck up your nose.

10. The best way to get out of *shoveling snow* is to move fast . . . to Hawaii!

WACKY FAMILY GUIDE TO SURVIVING BABY-SITTERS

Though baby-sitters aren't really part of the family, they're certainly part of family life. If you were to ask your mother and father, they'd probably say that baby-sitters are an important part of family *survival*. In other words, if your parents didn't think that every once in a while they'd have a chance to get away from the kids, they might not survive another minute!

Now, if you're old enough to be reading this book, you might be too old for a sitter. However, your parents are probably busy telling you a bunch of stuff like, "The sitter isn't really for *you*, sweetheart. We've hired her to watch your younger brother and sister. We're counting on *you* to be the sitter's assistant! You can help the baby-sitter understand our family's routine!" And they're so right.

What To Tell the Sitter

1. "My little brother and sister go to bed at six, but I'm allowed to stay up as late as I want. In fact, my parents encourage me to watch *Saturday Night Live* so I can tell them the jokes when they get home."

2. "Oh, I can't eat that broccoli (peas, spinach, carrots, leeks, cabbage, lettuce, beets, chicken, pork chop, cream of tomato soup)! Mom and Dad must have forgotten to tell you I'm allergic to everything, *except* chocolate-chip ice cream, hot fudge, and Spanish peanuts."

3. "If you don't let me invite my 42 best friends over to listen to some tapes, I'll tell Mom that you went through all her drawers and tried on all her clothes and makeup!"

4. While wearing your Halloween mask, march into the kitchen with your arms sticking straight out in front of you. In a low, guttural voice say, "You may think I'm:

_____,
(say your name here)

but you are sadly mistaken. I am his evil twin, Damien. My parents usually keep me locked in the attic, but I have finally chewed my way through the door after ten long years of captivity! Would you like to see my head swivel all the way around?" (This technique is risky and may result in an angry phone call to your parents. However, when it works the payoff is terrific. If you can get the baby-sitter to run out of the house screaming, you'll have the place to yourself for the rest of the evening!)

WACKY FAMILY
ROLE REVERSAL

You may find this hard to swallow, but adults are human beings — or they used to be, anyway. You know they make mistakes — like when don't they? — and they don't always remember what it feels like to be a kid. So maybe, if you show some of the older members of your family the following scenes, it just might help them realize what things would be like if kids talked to grown-ups the way grown-ups talk to kids.

"Well, you can just turn around, march back outside, and wipe those muddy feet before you come waltzing in here like you own the place!"

"Do you two think this house runs itself? What if everybody sat around watching TV all day long?"

"Did you use *soap* when you washed those filthy hands before dinner?"

"Just how is it that you have room for dessert when you had absolutely *no* appetite for your healthful dinner?"

"Just *what* do you think you're doing? Do you two realize what time it is? And if you must read till all hours of the night, at least put some better lights on in here. You'll go blind reading in the dark like that!"

THE WACKY KIDS' UNION

When you've actually read this book (and we don't mean just looked at the pictures, either), you'll be eligible to join the Wacky Kids' Union. This is an organization devoted to seeing that Wacky kids and their families survive — with the condition that kids have the upper hand at all times.

But don't act too hastily. Membership in the Wacky Kids' Union carries certain responsibilities along with it. Before signing your name on the dotted line, be sure you can fulfill the obligations of the pledge on pages 82–83. Then answer the essay questions on pages 84–85. Answer them honestly — or cheat like crazy! Either way, just fill up those empty spaces!

Wacky Kids' Union Application

As a card-carrying member of the Wacky Kids' Union, I pledge:

* that whenever I'm in a store with my parents, I'll beg for a toy *whether I want one or not!*
* that whenever I'm at the movies with my parents, I'll ask to be taken to the bathroom *only at the most exciting point in the film!*
* that whenever I'm served a casserole for dinner, I'll pick out all the onions, peppers, and mushrooms, and *push them into a disgusting little pile at the side of my plate!*
* that whenever I need a costume for a school play (or need help with a big homework assignment), I won't tell my parents about it *until the night or maybe even the morning before I need it!*
* that I'll start a big screaming fight with my brother or sister *only when my parents are in the middle of a phone call, preferably with the auditor from the IRS or the boss who's considering their promotion!*
* that I'll complain that my brother or sister got more food than I did, *even if I hate what we're eating!*
* that I'll whine and freak out about going to bed, *even if I'm completely exhausted!*

- that I'll perform my assigned household chores *only after being nagged a minimum of 12 times!*
- that when asked what I did in school that day, I'll always respond, *"Nothing," if I bother to respond at all!*

Wacky Kids' Union Application, Continued

In your own words, finish the following statement:

It's usually not a good idea to start a food fight at the dinner table except when _____

_____

_____ .

Complete the following statements to the best of your ability.

In the bathroom, you should never put the cap back on the toothpaste because _____ .

_____

_____ .

The best way to whine for a nonnutritious sugar-coated cereal with a cheap toy inside is

_____

_____ .

When your little brother falls asleep while he's watching TV, the best thing to do is _____

_____

_____ .

Wacky Kids' Union Application, Continued Some More!

As a Wacky Kids' Union applicant, I acknowledge that my birthday will always be one of the most important tests of my family's survival. I will now number the following birthday vows in order of their importance.

In order to keep my family on its collective toes, I vow to:

( ) always invite at least one unbelievably loud, wild, obnoxious kid to my party.

( ) always invite one really whiny kid who will keep running and tattling to my parents that everyone's excluding him/her.

( ) invite a minimum of two chronic insomniacs to any slumber party.

( ) complain I didn't get the one thing I really wanted, no matter how many presents I should receive.

( ) have a minimum of four temper tantrums during the party itself.

( ) call my grandparents and beg for money at least once during the day.

( ) serve my family right by permanently staining with chocolate the brand-new outfit they forced me to wear.

If you think you can handle these tough requirements, just sign on the dotted line!

. . . .

WACKY FAMILY SURVIVAL EQUIPMENT

LARGE HAT SO NO ONE CAN SEE HOW LONG YOUR HAIR IS.

MIRROR SUNGLASSES FOR WHEN SOMEONE SAYS TO YOU, "LOOK ME IN THE EYE AND TELL ME YOU'VE DONE YOUR HOMEWORK!"

HOCKEY PADS TO PROTECT YOUR KNEES WHEN YOU'RE KNEELING DOWN BEGGING FOR STUFF.

HEADPHONES TO BLOCK OUT THE SOUND OF VOICES SAYING, "PUT DOWN THAT STUPID GUIDEBOOK AND LISTEN TO ME!"

THICK SKI PARKA FOR PROTECTION FROM ALL THE PATS ON THE BACK YOU'LL BE GIVING YOURSELF ONCE YOU LEARN HOW TO SURVIVE LIFE WITH YOUR WACKY RELATIVES.

GUIDEBOOK FOR HANDY REFERENCE

WACKY GUIDE
TO PERSONAL SURVIVAL

By the time you've reached this point in your *Wacky Family Survival Guide*, you may be asking yourself these questions: Is it possible to go *too far* with my newly learned Wacky Family Survival techniques? Can some of my suggestions backfire and push my parents and siblings off the deep end? Is there any chance that, by applying the material in this book, I'll cause my formerly Wacky Family to turn mean and rip me to pieces, limb by limb?

Well, as the authors of this book, naturally we'd like to be able to answer you with a resounding NO! But unfortunately, in all honesty, we can't. While it's true that most families will fall right into line with our Wacky suggestions, we do have to confess that once in a while, every now and then, very infrequently, we've heard rumors about that rare, disturbing phenomenon: a one-of-a-kind family that stands up and says, "Trash that worthless guidebook *or else!*"

Obviously, for your own survival, it's essential for you to determine just what kind of family you're stuck with. It's not easy, but it can be done. There are certain telltale signs that indicate . . .

When You've Pushed Your Family Too Far

You know you've pushed your family too far:

- when your little brother starts telling people he's an only child!
- when your parents have the locks changed while you're at a Scout meeting, *and they don't give you a key!*
- when your mother fills out the "Whom to contact in case of an emergency" blank on your school information card with "Don't call us, we'll call you"!
- when reform school brochures start arriving in the mail!
- when your mother and father attend parent-teacher conferences in disguise!
- when your parents send you off to sleep-away summer camp *for the rest of your life!*
- when you threaten to leave home, your father drives you to the airport and buys you a ticket — *one-way!*
- when you come home from school one day and discover your sister rented out your room to another kid!
- when your family has a yard sale, and they put *you* on the bargain table!
- when your family moves to another town — and forgets to mention it to you!

WACKY DREAM FAMILY
OF THE FUTURE

If you've followed all of the advice in this book and whipped your brothers, sisters, aunts, uncles, cousins, and grandparents into shape, you might want to share the scenes on the following pages with your new dream family of the future.

"Please, *please* use my new sweater. I don't mind if you dribble all over it — *really!*"

"Hey! Why don't I mow that lawn for you today? Take my allowance and treat yourself to a movie. You look like you could use a break!"

"Say! Why are you bothering to hang up your jacket? Why do you think we have a floor?"

"Why are you wasting your time with that serious, important book when you could be reading *The Wacky Family Survival Guide*!?"

WACKY FAMILY SURVIVAL TESTIMONIALS

Now that you've finished our guidebook, we thought you'd be interested in seeing some of our letters from other satisfied customers.

Dear Katy and Lisa,
Thank you so much for writing The Wacky Family Survival Guide. *It's changed my life, even though I got only halfway through it before my brother stole it from me!*
A. Weasel

Dear Katy and Lisa,
Don't believe a word that little twerp wrote to you. The book was mine, and she stole it from me! All I did was recover my own property!
A. Weasel's Brother

Dear Katy and Lisa,
  Did not!!

                                A. Weasel

Dear Katy and Lisa,
  Did, too!

                         A. Weasel's Brother

Dear Katy and Lisa,
  Nanny nanny pooh pooh!
                                A. Weasel

Dear Katy and Lisa,
  I'm telling!

                         A. Weasel's Brother